Catching A Tiger By The Tail

By Angelo J. Bell
Published by Angelo J. Bell for CreateSpace and Amazon
Copyright 2018 Angelo J. Bell. All rights reserved.

Other books by Angelo:
The Gray Melia
A Perfect Weapon

~~~
**Dedicated To:**
Israel, Cimone, Zachary and Imara, the #Bell4Pack.
Nghia Nguyen, my true love, whether near or far.
Michael C. Cordell, friend, fellow writer and collaborator.
Erma, for graciously passing to me her love for writing.
Those mentioned herein for teaching me difficult lessons.
~~~


Chapter 1 – CATHING A TIGER BY THE TAIL
Chapter 2 – THAT TIME YOU WANT TO SLAP YOUR FRIEND AND HIS LAWYER
Chapter 3 – TALL FENCES MAKE GOOD NEIGHBORS – UNTIL THEY CLIMB OVER
Chapter 4 – SHOULD YOU ADAPT YOUR SCRIPT INTO A BOOK
Chapter 5 – NOW WE ARE FREE
Chapter 6 – GUN SHY NO MORE
Chapter 7 – DUDE, WERE WE IN THE SAME MEETING?
Chapter 8 – I SEE YOUR TRUE COLORS
Chapter 9 – DUDE, WE TALKED ABOUT THIS!
Chapter 10 – IDEAS ARE STILL IDEAL
Chapter 11 – TODAY

PREFACE

This book is comprised of several long-form posts from a blog I have been writing for over 10 years called (of many names), **Angelo Writes**. The post were written as a form of venting after I'd worked for over four years to secure my first pilot development TV writing deals. As the deals slowly came to fruition a funny, but no so funny thing happened. Money came into the equation and folks went nuts.

Even as I continued to think long term, as in, this was just a stepping stone towards a larger more fruitful landscape, my partners could not see beyond the horizon. It became a money-grab at all costs. Friendships were decimated. Opportunities were lost. Career were derailed.

I wrote the blogs to clear my mind, vent, scream and mostly to debrief for lessons-learned. Later, I began to realize that the lessons learned were important not just for me, but for my peers working in any and all areas of the entertainment business.

The need to write these blog posts and later assemble them into a book came after years of having people disappoint me. During my time of developing projects, pitches and films, I have helped hundreds of people in the entertainment biz. I have helped them pay their rent, build their reels, pad their resumes, win awards, revise their scripts, crowdsource their projects, market their endeavors, and essentially build their careers. Unfortunately I can literally count on one hand how many of their folks have returned the favor to me.

But this will not deter me. My character is to help, so I will continue to do so. Instead of stifling my desire to reach out and help I will simply choose your network of peers and teammates more wisely.

Lesson learned: Have a Plan. Follow your plan. Tell others your plan so that they are cognizant when they are intruding on your plan. Know that some folks will make excuses why they cannot help you but will have endless reasons why you should help them.

Most importantly, do not let bad experiences stop you. When people of questionable character knock you down or force you on a detour, adjust your sights, pick yourself up and just keep moving.

Thanks for reading. My blogs are located at http://www.AngeloJBell.com and http://AngeloBellWrites.Wordpress.com.

CATCHING A TIGER BY THE TAIL - IT CAN HURT

October 9, 2015

In the heat of July, I learned that I had not one, but **two TV development deals** in place with MajorTVNetwork affiliates. One deal was as the executive producer. The other deal was as writer, co-creator and exec-producer. This was the culmination of four years of working under a joint-venture between MajorTVNetwork and the Independent Film and Television Alliance (IFTA) to find new writing and producing talent to help revive the network.

Four years. It had been four years of pitching, working with a slew of close writer friends and then expanding that out to friends of friends, and then working with the Great American Pitchfest to open the door to anyone with a good idea. Unfortunately, it was also four years of hearing:

"No."

"Thanks but we have another project in development just like it."

"It's too dark for us."

"It's not edgy enough for us."

Four years of being the cheerleader for a bevy of writers and struggling to encourage them to have faith in the potential of the **tiger we had by the tail**. Four year of cheerleading despite hearing the above-mentioned versions of No, No and No.

Four years of wanting to give up, but deciding to give it another try, returning my creative thinking cap to my head and brainstorming another show idea -- for better or worse. Four years of watching the pool of producers engaged in this MajorTVNetwork/IFTA deal dwindle down from a few hundred to double-digits, and thinking, "Whew, I'm still in there."

Four years of learning that, although my production company, Kiss Hug Five Entertainment, hadn't achieved a win, our efforts were appreciated because we were bringing well-developed projects to the various networks. They liked us. They liked the writers. They liked **me**. Cool.

So, after four long years of pitching, when I learned that I had two projects in development with two networks I thought to myself, "This is it." I imagined walking around in a state of constant euphoria and bliss for all eternity, with a Cheshire cat smile on my face. I imagined being ridiculously happy from the inside out as I excitedly toiled with writing a pilot script for one network and guiding two writers to write a pilot script for a second network. Hell yeah, baby. This is what writing for TV is ALL about!

Wrong. There was no euphoria. No blinding bliss. No true collaboration. No love. No respect. No gratitude. Instead, this has been the most frustrating, chaotic, and the darkest time since I stepped into the independent writer/filmmaker ring nearly fifteen years ago. **This experience has single-handedly changed the way I create and do business**. Forever. I have never been so angry with people in my life. I have never been so surprised and disappointed in people's behavior since my divorce. I have never, ever wanted to quit this business as much as I have wanted to quit over the last four months.

However, yesterday, Thursday October 8th, I had a long overdue conversation with Dionna, someone I met during brighter aspects of the past four years, and she reminded me of something very important. Four years ago, I hated pitching. I loathed it to the point where I would sooner be told NO through email, than sit in a pitch meeting. However, I went from loathing pitching to fine-tuning the art of my pitch and the pitches of those I worked with so I could go into any room and dazzle the shit out of the person on the other side of the table.

She reminded me that I went from being deathly afraid of pitching to breaking it down to a science that corrals my fears (I still have them) and unleashes that angst in a manner that helps the storytelling. Dionna reminded me that I went from being a newbie at MajorTVNetwork, to having the telephone numbers of key department heads in my contact list with open invitations to come back and pitch again. I scored more pitch meetings in the first six months of 2015, than in the previous 3 1/2 years combined.

I was reminded that this business is a series of processes. Pitching was a process I had to master the same way a director has to master his interaction and communication with people on a film set. Now I have to master this dark side, this Dark Force, if you will, that surfaces when you start talking deals, collaborations, Agreements, division of responsibilities and of course, money.

Dionna told me, "You've got to write a blog post about this, Angelo. You've been through it and you're still here. Tell people what to expect." She was right. **People should know what to expect. I'll be blogging about it in a series of posts for the rest of the year.** In order to show people fully what to expect, I must include things I did wrong as well as things I did right. I have to include my shortcomings, hindsight revelations, blindness, naïveté, stupidity and the warning signals I ignored.

Speaking of my Atlanta friend, Dionna, her friendship is one of two indisputably AMAZING friendships I've clung to over the last four years (see, it wasn't all bad, ha-ha).

Dionna and my good friend, road-dog, sister-from-another-mister and pitching partner **Ramona** have been instrumental in keeping me in this game called **show business**. More than once I've called/texted/Messengered them to talk me off the ledge. They did. They have kept me sane. So while the next 2 1/2 months will be filled with the juicy bullshit that has happened, there will also be sprinklings of amazing things that have happened to me as well. As I said, before - If you don't have anything good to say, why say anything at all.

WHEN YOU REACH THAT POINT WHEN YOU WANT TO BITCH-SLAP YOUR EX-FRIEND AND HIS LAWYER

October 16, 2015

There was no euphoria. No blinding bliss. No true collaboration. No love. No respect. No gratitude. Instead, this has been the most frustrating, chaotic, and the darkest time since I stepped into the independent writer/filmmaker ring nearly fifteen years ago. **This experience has single-handedly changed the way I create and do business.** Forever.

I wrote *this* post last week, on October 9, 2015, immediately after my first blog post about the state of affairs regarding my immersion onto dual TV development deals with MajorTVNetwork. I hastily made the decision to start blogging about this after I received a phone call from MajorTVNetwork Business Affairs.

Houston, we have a problem!

But allow me to back-up to give you a more complete and picturesque view of the situation.

When someone boldly and without solicitation mentions his or her longstanding relationship with an entity you're conducting business with -- be-fucking-ware. It means they are already diminishing your relationship in their mind and may possibly seek to outwardly derail or discredit you in the future to preserve his or her sake of self-importance.

Friday, October 9, 2015 I check my voicemail and I have two messages from the Business Affairs division of

MajorTVNetwork. Odd. The last time I spoke with this particular rep was when I was finalizing the agreement between MajorTVNetwork and my production company, Kiss Hug Five Entertainment, and the Agreement between me and the writing team. My mind immediately started to whirl. There had been signs from the get-go that this was going to be a tenuous collaboration despite that fact that I brought these two writers to the deal, the money and the opportunity. Without me they had nothing. Their previous general meetings by agents had been fruitless. All talk. In fact, I wasn't even looking for projects to pitch at the time. I was done with collaborations. But one of the writers, a friend and industry colleague, came to me. I used my connections, contacts and relationship to get the pitch meeting and the resulting deal.

There is an old saying, "Don't bring a knife to a gunfight." I should have seen the signs on the wall from day one. That was my naïveté. It's where and when I blew it. See, when the development deal for the second cable network came down it happened with a close colleague, for whom I'd already gotten two pitch meetings. When this third meeting resulted in a deal for him and his writing partner I thought we'd proceed as friends. They didn't think so. They brought in a lawyer who viewed me as an adversary. My friend's sudden unavailability and supposed ineffectiveness at managing his lawyer's and partner's actions proved problematic. Ultimately they effectively they caused an unnecessary three-week delay in signing the contracts.

From the start the lawyer and the writing partner seemed perturbed that, I (Kiss Hug Five Entertainment) was in the midst of this deal. These parties seemed miffed that the network recognized ME as the intermediary and facilitator. They didn't have carte blanche to do whatever they wanted; each iteration of story development had to go through me. I sensed a desire to leapfrog over me although this was, by its very nature, an option deal.

Writers come to me with a concept. I help them hone the project and bring everyone to the network with myself attached as producer. The network likes it, pays and I am inextricably attached. Simple. I made no attempt to change the story or finagle my way onto the writing team. I was, by **contract**, a Non-writing producer. Period. But my involvement did not sit well with team's lawyer. I'm sure he sat down and said, "Who the fuck is this guy?"

I'm the fucking guy who had a relationship with the network, got you a seat at the table and put a five-figure deal in your lap.

I'm not paranoid. Well, at least I wasn't back then. However, when I am the executive producer of the project and I ask the writers to send the outline they're working on, and they respond, "We're keeping that information close to the vest," there's something fishy in Fishkill.

BACK TO SCENE: It's October 9, and I'm talking to the Business Affairs rep and, lo and behold, the writing team's lawyer has lodged a complaint about payment terms and now he wants me removed from the payment equation. That is to say, the Network pays my production company and my production company pays the writers. I don't lose any money and the terms are same. But, the writer's lawyer wants MajorTVNetwork to pay the writer directly. As far as I can tell, it's a step to kick me to the curb...an action taken by my friend's lawyer. Hmmm... so what's my role again?

My second mistake was not getting a full rundown of the payment process from MajorTVNetwork. There is where I made a mistake. But between friends, it's like, hey, the money is there, you just have to wait 30 days. Not so with a lawyer, especially when the writers conveniently hide behind him. "Oh, we leave all the money matters to our lawyer. We just want to focus on the creative." Cough*cough*bullshit*cough.

Still, the lawyer -- who boldly professed his in-depth, longstanding business relationship with MajorTVNetwork -- wasn't aware of these terms either. Or perhaps he made an assumption, or simply tried to dupe me. Either way, the stage had been set for contention.

I remind people that a Teddy Bear is still a bear. I may be a Teddy Bear, but when you push me into a corner, threaten my credibility, fuck with my money, or condescend, my bear claws come out. It's not a side of me you want to see and not a side I want to show. It ain't pretty and I try real hard to keep that bear in hibernation. Suffice it to say that my first inkling was to tell everyone to go fuck his or herself, while in the back of my mind I relished the thought of bitch-slapping the lawyer upon a random and coincidental meeting.

A phrase uttered by Vin Diesel as Riddick in **Pitch Black** comes to mind:

> https://www.youtube.com/watch?v=TBEmcIuGLTc

But I digress...

My gut had always told me that this team wanted to leapfrog over me and eliminate me from the equation. In the beginning there was this, "Who are you again?" reaction, as if they'd suddenly and spontaneously made the connection and introduction to MajorTVNetwork execs on their own. WTF.

To my detriment, I stupidly sat back and said very little as their lawyer took three weeks to "rewrite" a contract that was already written. I sat back and said nothing when I should have called bullshit. One person hid behind the lawyer, the other person hid behind the other writer. No one was culpable. It was a neat trick. Still, I looked to the bigger picture. Get this show into pilot phase. Get this show on the air and all the bullshit means nothing.

However, on October 9, 2015 it all became clear. It was a slap in the face that I took like a punch from Mike Tyson in his prime. I pulled into the parking lot of the Cerritos Public Library, sat in my car and listened to the Business Affairs rep. She was cool, but there was an issue and MajorTVNetwork needed to resolve it. As it turned out, the very thing the writers set their lawyer out to get took a huge amount of stress off my shoulders.

But, it was still fucked up that they went there, but in the end, the problem was now MajorTVNetwork's, not mine. What hurt most was that something else was very clear: There was no gratitude for what I put together for these folks. There was no recognition of my contribution in this opportunity. It was simply a matter of folks going after all they can, by any means necessary, and I was standing in the way.

I've been at this for a very long time. Four years of developing contacts, friends and supporters at MajorTVNetwork. I already know what I have to do. If the deal goes through and we go to pilot I will executive produce the shit out of that series. I'll also work on other projects that mean more to me. If this project dies -- well, it stops there. The project stays in development hell and I still move on to greener pastures. I have to say thanks to the asshole lawyer because his initial attempts to leapfrog over me bought me a new car. Either way, when this is done, it'll be dead-and-done.

TALL FENCES MAKE GOOD NEIGHBORS

October 24, 2015

Tall fences make good neighbors -- right up until the time they realize it doesn't take much energy to climb over and start playing in your grass...and fucking everything up in the process.

I must preface this post. Before you read, I must admit something: everything I outline here, in the next few words, **is entirely my fault.** This instance of an addition to the cavalcade of false ride-or-die mofos tossing knives at my 12th vertebrae came as a result of my blind inaction. I was naive. I kept leaning into the jab instead of running from it. The blame rests with me.

Imagine, if you will, four years of coming to the rescue of an aspiring TV producer, who was an idea man. That is to say, he could bullshit his way through a show concept but had no professional writing skills to execute his ideas. Imagine, throughout the years you never hear from this guy until needs a one-sheet, or a pitch book, or even a script. He can't pay you but promises, "If this show takes off, I'm going to take care of you." You say, "Cool," and you write a 35-page script for a submission to HBO and Showtime, or a fifth one-sheet, or a complete character outline.

The years of "friendship" with this gentleman are full of pleas for help with concepts. Most concepts are for reality shows, which admittedly aren't your forte, but you press on. You write. You deliver each and every time you are asked.

Now imagine this guy, let's call him Greg, calls you up with an idea for a reality show. He needs a pitch proposal. You write it. However, somewhere during your conversation you realize that this reality show would be a kick-ass scripted show. So you pitch that to him. He bites. Then you request time go into your bat cave and write it. You do. You come back with a fully conceived idea for a night-time soap/drama. Unfortunately, despite the work you've put in, and despite the dude's lack of skills at developing stories and characters, he wants to change everything you put together. So you change it, but you keep your logline the same. That's the essence of the show. You submit the logline to your contacts and WHAM! You get a pitch meeting.

You break it down and tell Greg the way it works. My contact, my company has the first look deal with the network, I will exec produce, I will write the pilot (since you are not a writer) and you retain exec producer and creator status.

It was simple. Unfortunately, **everything** that Greg changed in the pitch proposal is what the network executive finds fault with. Plus there is an air of authenticity thee network wants. You are given a second chance. You go back to the drawing board. You reach out to your old 9-5 contacts. Someone who now runs all U.S. offices of a multi-million dollar Fortune 500 company. She is so cool with you, that when you ask for her help, she invites you into her executive boardroom and basically promises to engage her top people to help you with anything you want for the show. SCORE!

You go back for the second meeting with the network locked-and-loaded. But something is different. Greg is now acting like your contact at the network is his contact. He's sending emails without your consent. Whoa! The network passes on the project.

Then you get sick. You spend a month in the hospital and while that's happening, Greg uses information you provided to finagle his way into this IFTA deal. Becoming a part of IFTA is not a big deal, but he deliberately kept his intent from you. Why?

So, now Greg is in the TV business with you. Still, he's not a writer, nor can he usher a concept through development. He's a formula guy. He sees everything as paint by the numbers. He doesn't appreciate the craft and art behind writing. He doesn't realize that painting-by-numbers will never give you a Picasso.

So, it's been four years of writing one-sheets, proposals, a script and polishing poorly written work given to Greg by "writers" he trusted. Then you got him his first Network tv pitch meeting. And as a result you gave him access to this world to pitch TV. What has he done for you in return? Jack. Shit.

But all that is about to change. He comes to you with an idea. It's half an idea but you see something in it. You agree to develop it as co-creator, pitch it through his company with you attached as the writer and co-creator. Simple. You write another pitch proposal. Greg jumps in and wants to change things. Again. You change them but warn him against making the show to formulaic. He can't comprehend that because he's a paint-by-number producer (if you can call him that).

You go into the meeting, pitch the idea and BITCH SLAP. Everything you warned Greg about is what the network dislikes. It's a very bad meeting. The executive has stopped taking notes, has slammed his pen down and is either glaring at you or rolling his eyes. You and Greg are getting your asses handed to you. The answer from the network isn't simply "No," it's more like, "No, and what the hell were you thinking!" You've tuned out and you just want to go home. Greg is quiet. He can't even talk anymore. It's been a long day. The meeting is over. Done.

But the network exec says something, gives you an opening, and you have a lightbulb moment. You wing it. Ad lib. No net. No prep.

"What if we wrote the show like this...?"

The exec picked up his pen. He likes that idea. Keep going, he says, You wing it some more. Ideas forming and spreading at the speed of thought. They like it. They want to take that idea to the higher ups. Success.

Here's where he starts climbing fences.

A week later, the network comes back. They love the idea, and they want to move forward with development. Without any prodding they immediately recognize **me** as the writer. **Why not?** They've known me and my production company Kiss Hug Five Entertainment through four years of pitching.

There's money coming to... the writer. The Producer/Production company has to negotiate its own deal.

But Greg says, he wants to bring in some "experienced" writers to "help our chances." He's starts quoting magazine articles about the writers and showrunners for the new season and how they all have history with the network.

Crazy-lying-sonuvabitch-says-what?

Money popped into the equation and now he wants to change things to give himself access to the money, although he is not a writer. I tell him, you'll never be able to hire an established writer with that money because it's a mere pittance to them. He won't relent but learns he cannot hire another writer because the network has to approve all writers. So he changes gears. It's no longer about tilting the odds in our favor by hiring an established TV writer. Now, he figures, is as good a time as any to learn the process of writing. Soooo, despite the fact that he can't even **say** "manipulate" much less spell it, he's going to step in as writer since he's already approved.

What. The. Fuck. Squared.

So we went from Greg believing we needed an experienced TV writer/showrunner in order to compete, to Greg placing his no-talent-ass in the equation as writer. Makes no goddamn sense at all. But why did he do it? For two reasons: 1) The Money 2) He knew I wouldn't allow a poor script with my name on it to go to the network so I will rewrite as necessary.

He weaseled his way over onto my side of the fence to play in my yard. And then things really get downright ridiculous.

NOW WE ARE FREE: Tall Fences Make Good Neighbors, Part II

October 30, 2015

To backtrack, I introduce this guy into the process, he misappropriated my contacts, manipulates my good nature, suckers me into a corner and steals my ideas.... now, where were we? Oh yeah. My dunce cap...

Last episode we'd just gotten the network deal to develop/write an outline for the pilot script. Money popped into the equation and my non-writing partner opted to jump over into my side of the fence (writing arena), basically for a payday, without considering the larger picture. I was prepared and willing to do all of the writing and even split the fee if he would just leave me alone to write. Ultimately we could have a show on the air if he'd just let me do what I do! He didn't.

I was pissed, so I stepped away and started working on the outline for the pilot. I don't take his calls, I just work. A week before the pilot outline is due we finally speak. Lo and behold, Greg has gone and written an outline too! Really? I'm shocked, so I asked to read the outline.

Remember what I said about Greg being a paint-by-numbers guy?

Three pages in, I say to myself, "Greg **did not** write this outline. He had help." Greg knows nothing about screenplay format, but the outline he submitted shows awareness of format and structure. Unfortunately, the outline is one huge derivative mess. It's merely a bunch of scenes tossed together without any connection, build-up, drama or conflict. Worse, the scene that should have started the story comes at the very last minute when it should have been the first scene. It was awful. I told Greg his outline was merely a collection of random scenes tossed together. There was no story. No beginning, middle or end. No Act breaks, no cliffhangers, nada. He disagreed, but he alluded to the idea that whatever was wrong *I* could fix it for him since I was the better writer. Hmmm.

It didn't stop there. Greg didn't like my outline because, "It didn't have enough characters and it was too focused on the two main characters." Yeah, you read that right. Not enough characters, and my two main characters had too much screen time. WTF?! He thought that by simply adding more characters the show would automatically be amazing like **Empire** or **unRea**l. Forget about the great writing that is attributed to the success of these shows. To him, it's all about the number of characters on the show. God help me.

So now that Greg has read **my** outline he starts rewriting his outline -- by stealing elements of my story and structure. I start to see TRANSITIONS, SCENE HEADINGS and SUPERS in his outline that weren't there before. Remind you, he's a paint-by-the-numbers guy. He thinks there's a magic bullet or tried and true **formula for everything**. IF YOU ADD TRANSITIONS AND CHARACTERS, AND BORROW FROM TOP SHOWS, THE SHOW WILL BE GREAT.

Oh, and let me remind you, our story included a love story between the two main characters who are mentioned in the logline (which never changed). In Greg's outline he made one of those characters gay. Not both. Just one.

AGAIN, I told Greg everything that was wrong with his story outline. He still believed his outline was better than mine. I barely got him to admit that someone else helped him write his outline, but he wouldn't say who wrote it. I took my outline off the table and told him to submit his outline. He did.

Network called back to schedule a conference call to give us notes -- only, they **didn't** give us notes. They DROP-KICKED THE SHIT OUT HIS OUTLINE. They did it very politely and very sweetly by saying, "We cannot give you notes because so much needs to change, it's like you have to rewrite everything." Oh, and the things they disliked about Greg's outline were exactly the things I told him were wrong.

Back to the drawing board. TIME LOST: 2 MONTHS

Now, if that was me getting my concept drop-kicked, I would have apologized to my partners and promised to humble myself. Greg never did. In fact I don't think he realized that when a network exec cannot give you notes on your outline it's because the outline is horrible. Period. He started coming up with even more lame ideas to cram into the show. I was dumbfounded. I sat their thinking," Weren't you on the same conference call as I?"

I decided to placate Greg by taking some of the elements of his outline and mold them into my original concept. I thought, if I included some of his ideas (and made them workable) he'd STFU and let me write. For two weeks I come home after a 13-hour work day and write for 3 hours. I crafted a 35-page outline for a one-hour dramedy and polished it down to 27 pages. We were a week late on delivery but it was finally ready. Greg calls and says, "Let's bounce some ideas around."

Bounce some ideas around? Bro, we are a **week late**. The time to "bounce ideas around" has come and gone. I'd repeatedly asked him to submit his ideas to me by email. But email requires writing and Greg sucks at ANY FORM

OF WRITING. He cannot put together a cohesive, coherent sentence without spelling errors and poor grammar unless he cuts & pastes it from another source. I always knew this about him and that's why he would always send his emails to me to correct before he sent them to a network person.

I reminded him that if we bounce ideas around we're going to have to rewrite the outline. No, make that *I* am going to have to rewrite the outline, and I am ready to put this thing to bed. Then he starts telling me some ideas he had to change things. Things that, as he put it, "Will make the **storytelling better**." Was he really about to make the same mistake again? Could he be that blind? That stupid? That arrogant?

Yes. He was.

Whoever he trusted with helping him write the outline failed miserably. Now here he was again, trying to compare his no talent, no experience, no respect, non-writing asshole (and that of his secret source) with me. I told him that it was disrespectful to all the writers who slave for years over screenplays for him to think he could waltz in with no background or training and write a professional quality pilot screenplay and outline. I told him he had no respect for the art and craft. No respect for the sacrifice. I've spent over three decades improving my craft and I'll take criticism from anyone who put in at least that much dedication to the art and craft of writing. But not from him.

I was pissed. I was livid. He was putting the kibosh our show and didn't even know it. I called him every profane name I could think of calling him. I had violent thoughts. I wanted to reach down his little throat, into his little 5'6" body and rip out his gonads and pull them out through his nose. I was done with this fucker! And so I said "Fuck you!" -- and I submitted my outline to the network. Yup. I did that.

And guess what? They called back and were excited to finally have a new outline. But the story doesn't end there.

Greg (whose real name is Greg, by the way) contacted the network after he secretly rewrote the outline behind my back and submitted his revision as an update to my outline. When I sent my outline to the network I copied Greg on the email. He didn't have the balls to do that. As usual he made his moves stealthily. I only learned he'd replaced my outline on the very day we were supposed to have the conference call with the network about the outline. He sends me an email stating, "I've been trying to get in contact with you..."

Trying to get in contact with me? Funny. My email address hasn't changed. I've had the same email address for over ten years. I received no email from you, Greg. You obviously weren't trying very hard.

Obviously he got help, again, to rewrite my outline. Obviously he piggy-packed off my work -- again -- because his work was subpar. Obviously he hadn't learned from having his previous outline drop kicked by the network.

Can you guess what the outcome was? **The network passed on the project**. Again. We had a five-step deal and it died right there.

Twice Greg would not let me do that thing that I do without interruption. Twice he fell short trying to do it his way. His touch is the touch of death and it killed this project that had so much potential. The money was killed; there were no fees for writing an outline, script and rewrites. The possibility of writing a script for a major cable network was killed. The deal was killed. The potential of having an award-winning show on TV...was killed. But the worst part of everything is: Greg still didn't grasp the fact that he killed our deal because of his greed.

Yes, I am disappointed about the deal and the potential opportunity. Inside I am crushed that all this work bears so little fruit. However, I am extremely happy to be done with this dickhead once and for all.

It's done. To quote Juba from GLADIATOR, "Now we are free."

SHOULD YOU ADAPT YOUR SCREENPLAY INTO A NOVEL?

Let's back up a second....

March 5, 2015

I continue to mull over the idea of tackling a novel this year by adapting one of my scripts. My first thought was to take the journey with an epic fantasy love story, LEGEND OF BLACK LOTUS, which made the top 15% of Nichols Fellowship in 2012 and Scriptapalooza said "...script excels on every level." Now I'm considering my contemporary neo noir action thriller, A PERFECT WEAPON, that one pro script reader compared to the Cohen Bros' NO COUNTRY FOR OLD MEN in her coverage. The idea of being able to include ALL the vast story elements I had to remove from each script is intoxicating. Decisions. Decisions.

I reached out to my friend, Michael C Cordell who is an author and screenwriter for advice. He, is one of the few folks out there who has read both of the scripts in question. Below is the very thorough advice Michael passed on to me:

Absolutely, I agree, do it!

There are so many elements that can't be shown on the screen that a narrative vehicle like a novel can provide. A screenwriter's challenge is to adequately demonstrate the thoughts and intentions of the characters on the screen, aside from narration and direct exposition; it's very much a challenge. Of course, some stories don't need to explore the inner dialog of the characters, either.

Your neo-noir action thriller works as a film because of the vividness of the screenwriting. However, you can add a lot of texture in a novelization and it may end up altering the screenplay after all is said and done.

The great thing about a novel, besides exploring the inside world of the characters, is you get to really expand on descriptions of the story world where in screenplays, you need to be sparse in order to fit the entire work into an acceptable length. It's an opportunity to explore your creation from the ground up and with a new set of eyes.

Advice #1: Read the novel Old Country for Old Men and compare it to the shooting script (I'm sure it can be found). It may sound obvious, but you may be able to better understand what the reader was seeing when she read your script. I know you're going script-to-novel vs. the other way, but I think it'll be a good exercise anyway.

Advice #2 & #3: Either begin with an existing outline or begin outlining using the current script as your source. A relatively small investment in a product called Scrivener (for both Mac & PC, by the way) is definitely worth it. I use it almost exclusively for writing screenplays, novels, even short stories. It helps me organize my thoughts, my scene management, character and scene descriptions, etc. The bonus: it's relatively inexpensive compared to other writing software and pays for itself years after you buy it.

(Note: Literature & Latter, the makers of Scrivener, have yet to release an IOS version of the product, despite years of development and announcements of "It's coming." They promise it'll be out this year ... I'm not convinced.)

So, in light of the fact that I prior to Feb 2015 I hadn't read a novel since The MockingJay, but I've just finished a

Michelle Perry romance thriller novel, Paint it Black, I officially toss my hat into the ring. My script A PERFECT WEAPON will be adapted into a crime thriller in the vein of...you guessed it, NO COUNTRY FOR OLD MEN with a little THE FUGITIVE mixed in.

GUN SHY NO MORE

November 3, 2015

A reference to the rise of the Phoenix from the ashes would be too corny right now. Add to that a reference to the Fiery Phoenix of G-Force and man, talk about overkill. But both are very appropriate, depending on your perspective.

If anyone ever wanted to do a background check on me it's pretty easy. Just come to my blog, check me out on YouTube, or my Facebook account. It's easy to uncover how many films I've made, screenplays I've written, awards won, TV pitches I've attended (on both sides of the table), how many deals translated into dollars and how many people I've helped get their first meeting with a network TV executive. Simple. I love producing. I love creating. My passion is manifest in my 30 year history as a writer, and 15 years as a filmmaker. If anyone ever attempts to cast shade on me, check the playback. It's all there.

But 2015 has been a helluva year! :(

It's been filled with good, bad and ugly. I've been looking forward to that Midnight Hour coming of grace and favor for a few months now. More than anything, I've wanted to produce again. However, the last year has made me gun shy. But no more.

A new project has lifted me out of the ashes of BS, greed, backstabbing and ungratefulness. Like the Fiery Phoenix, I have a new mission that returns me to independent filmmaking. The writer of this project and I are working out the details of an Agreement for both film and TV. Yes, there will be a written agreement. The motion picture project that results, regardless of the medium, is going to be spectacular. At this point all I can say is the film version is like **EVE'S BAYOU** meets **THE BIG CHILL**. And, what **WINTER'S BONE** did for Jennifer Lawrence and John Hawkes, **this indie film** will do for some young actors.

Unlike my most recent project with a co-producer, the writer of this project is **a true writer**. She is a student of her craft, a lover of the art of screenwriting, and someone who respects and honors the process. And she is a fair business woman who ultimately see the endgame: TV. Movies. Distribution. Broadcast. Residuals.

I'm going to be directing and producing this amazing film (if the stars line up), or executive producing an even more amazing miniseries. So yes, I am rising up out of the ashes just like the **Phoenix**. Who cares if it sounds corny? :)

WTF DUDE?! WEREN'T WE IN THE SAME MEETING?

November 6, 2015

One of the scariest things about having co-anything is the difference in perspectives. Notice I did not say difference in opinions. Different opinions are expected, but aren't perspectives about interpreting something based on fact and tangible data? Unfortunately, in the world of screenwriting and producing for television, people's personal experiences and lack of knowledge (or talent) can often get in the way.

If you look to the sky while visiting Zimbabwe you'll say the sky is blue if asked. You'd probably say the same thing (minus some cloud cover colors) if you were in England, Cairo, Sante Fe, Barranquilla, Antarctica or The Netherlands. When someone starts saying the sky is red -- and you're looking at the same damn sky -- it's time to prepare for the Zombie Apocalypse or schedule a 5150 on your friend. Shit has gotten real and that fucker is insane!

Seriously though, differences in perspectives happen all the time, mostly in varying but manageable degrees. A West Coast writer might see things differently than an East Coast Writer. However, in a worst case scenario things can deteriorate rapidly. At its worst, your partners will begin to see and interpret behavior and statements in a meeting that were never there to begin with. These are things their psyche has implanted into the equation simply because they want it to be so.

What the hell does this mean? It's easier if I give you an example.

I was once on a conference call with a partner. We listened to the Development Manager at the network discuss the needs of the network, its brand, and similar shows. This network doesn't do action, supernatural or any kind of sci-fi. The network's meat-and-potatoes is drama geared towards women 18-45. However, the network mentioned a show on its sister network called COVERT AFFAIRS. I've watched CV since its pilot and I like everything about the show. But, like its name suggests, it's a spy drama. Well, the Development Manager mentioned COVERT AFFAIRS and how the lead character has to manage a double life. She's a spy for the CIA and she's regular Jane. The show dabbles in all the challenges she faces dealing with having an alternate identity.

Okay, got it. The project we were pitching involved a woman with a similar identity crisis, but our show was solidly based in reality. Definitively, it is a relationship drama, definitely NOT an action drama.

Unfortunately, after the meeting, as I debriefed with my so-called partner, he started prattling on about how the network wanted us to make... **a spy show**.

Huh? What? Wait... were we on the same conference call? What the f*ck are you talking about?

Then he goes on to talk about all the shows the Development Manager mentioned and how we should incorporate ALL (not some) of those elements into our show. I sat back in amazement at how he made the reference fit neatly into the numbskull idea he wanted to pursue.

It's like someone using excerpts from The Bible - taken out of context - to fit their own personal twisted mean-spirited agenda, and then say, "It's God's plan."

The Manager mentioned CUPID. It's a show that originated in Canada starring Jeremy Piven (Entourage) in 1998 and was revised in 2009 with Bobby Cannavale at the helm. Considering our topic, the show was right-on! Unfortunately my partner didn't care for the show because he didn't understand the humor. So, despite those intense similarities in our relationship drama he totally overlooked this reference. Instead he focused on **Unreal**, a pseudo reality show drama about the BS that goes on with shows like **The Bachelor** and The **Bachelorette** (I admit it, watching **Unreal** is like being hypnotized by a train wreck - I cannot turn away). But our show was nothing like Unreal. His thought process went like this:

Oh wait, UNREAL is a behind the scenes matchmaking show. Let's use that idea as a mashup between it, MILLION DOLLAR MATCHMAKER and SCANDAL and we've got a hit show!

Ugh. Time for me to eat my gun. Everything he did and said exasperated me.

I tried convincing him that we had a relationship dramedy more closely related to CUPID and MOONLIGHTING, with its biting sarcasm, commentary on relationships, and back-n-forth interplay between two main characters. Ultimately we want the audience to cheer for them to get together, like Maddy and Addison. Lois & Clark, Tony and Angela (**Who's The Boss**).

Nope.

Fuck it. I skipped ahead. Maybe this show gets better in the Second Act, I thought to myself. But I made the mistake of telling him to rewatch the first 15 minutes of EMPIRE. He's not a writer so I need to show him a visual of how a well-written First Act sets everything up and introduces all the major players. Damn. Stupid move, Angelo. There's nothing scarier than hearing someone say,

"Oh, no I've got it," And then the next sentence out of their mouth proves they don't got it. End result: dude wanted to change our romantic dramedy into some sort of EMPIRE-ish pop culture drama.

I tried hard to get him back on track.

Dude! We pitched a **romantic dramedy** series. Are you sure you were in the same meeting as I?

I kept going back to the discussion we had with the development executive during the conference call. Even though I could recall what the exec said, almost verbatim, it didn't matter. My so-called producing partner had his own agenda and everything was twisted to fit his plan. He was pulverizing round pegs into fine powder and dumping it into a square hole.

I should have paid closer attention to the signs. My non-writing, producing partner had already started to climb over the fence and shit in my yard. You can imagine what ultimately happened to the project.

I SEE YOUR TRUE COLORS...AND THEY SUCK

November 13, 2015

I've seen and heard just about everything in the 4 years I've been pitching TV, the 10 years I've been making indie films and the [mumbles] years I've been writing. One of the most ironic things I've heard is an admonishment about networking from a writer who benefited from **my network**.

After getting this gentleman a network pitch meeting, **twice** -- something one of his supposed agent friends couldn't do (they just got him a general meeting), he came to me with a third project. At the time I was focused on working and developing my projects alone. The headache and heartache of dealing with writers and their ups & downs, lack of commitment, and poor follow-through was disturbing. I'd seen one too many people appear hyper-excited about something they'd written (and rightfully so) only to basically close shop and move on after the first "No" from the network. I'd seen this phenomenon in the indie film arena with actors and directors. I had no intention of continuing to beat my head against a rock.

But, this guy was one of those peeps who had kept working. Unlike many of the writers I'd worked with, I didn't need to prod him for content and he kept in contact with anything he was working on. I took that as a good sign. As reluctant as I was to work with someone outside the family, I agreed to work with him and his new writing partner. We had to fine-tune the synopsis for a sitcom that would also work as a dramedy for the right network. They didn't have a workable logline so I coached and nudged them through writing a snappy logline that conveyed the essence of the show's drama and comedy. The end result: we got a deal to develop and write a pilot script for the network.

LESSON LEARNED: When your friend, colleague, partner, bro, bruh or homie hires a lawyer, **you had better hire a lawyer too**.

My "friend's" writing partner hired a lawyer to handle their interests in the deal I'd brokered with the TV network. The lawyer turned out to be a dickwad who thought that he could fire-off a sternly written email -- about damn near anything -- and I'd jump through hoops to pacify him. Fuck that. To his diabolical credit, he'd cleverly changed wording in the contract in the area of payment. To my detriment, I allowed it to happen. But everyone knew the network was funding the project, right? If we had to wait 30 days to get a five-figure check, no big deal, right?

Then my friend would hide behind his lawyer and his writing partner whenever I tried to get answers. He said he didn't want to deal with the money side. "Let the lawyer handle that." But I told him I'd be sending all updates to him directly. Screw the condescending son-of-a-bitch lawyer.

Do you know what my friend said to me?

He said, "This business is about relationships. And technically you're in breach of contract if you do that. I'd hate to see you strain relationships with people in the business."

What. The. Fuck.

I was on the phone at the time, goggled-eyed and incredulous. "Breach of contract? I'm putting $$ in your pocket. What the fuck are you talking about?" I said to myself. "This is your **lawyer**. This guy isn't a producer or a network executive. Basically, he's my sworn enemy, trying to take from me and give to you. Our relationship is organically combative. Why would I give a shit if I burn bridges with him? If I never come into contact with him again, it'll be completely fine."

My mind was blown. But the die was cast. He'd shown me his true colors. He'd say anything to leverage his side. He'd have me chugging absinthe and singing kumbaya with his lawyer if it meant that his cup runneth over -- at my expense. His reaction was absurd because everything was already set in stone. The deal, the contracts, the network's involvement. **Everything** was already agreed upon. What difference would it truly make if I sent updates about the payment schedule to him directly instead of to his lawyer?

This showed me that all his previous excuses about staying away from the money talk was bullshit. It was simply his way of deferring responsibility for his earlier haggling, which set us back three weeks. Money causes people to show their ass. Toss money into the equation and people become dumb with a fear factor that is multiplied to the nth degree. That's when people really start acting ridiculously stupid, and true colors shine through.

The other thing that pissed me off was that he dared to attempt to school me on the benefits of networking. I was not some 0-year producing neophyte. I've been in this game for a long time, and I've pitching for 4 years --- with 10 other writers, long before **he** came along.

Ungrateful son-of-a-bitch.

But **true colors** are like stains you can't scrub away. I am a firm believer that money cannot put anything inside of you **that isn't already there**. So, three cheers for deception, manipulation, dishonesty and for being a fraud, and for sucking as a friend.

DUDE, WTF! WE TALKED ABOUT THIS!

November 20, 2015

In the pitching world there is nothing more soul-sucking that a pitch meeting that goes completely awry. Sometimes the network exec is simply having a bad day, some execs always have a bad day and sometimes, **you** have a bad day. All you can do is prepare, roll with the brutal punches and scurry away with your tail between your legs to pitch another day.

I know this because I've done some scurrying in my time. In fact, I completed an entire year of scurrying. I say I have been pitching networks for over four years. That is not an entirely accurate statement. It has been four years; however, the first year of pitching was all done in written form. I did not meet with a single network executive. **I did not want to meet with a network executive**. I was too scared.

I spent the first year of pitching in my office developing full-blown concepts, pitch documents, pitch books, treatments, outlines and summaries. I made everything as in-depth and thorough as possible. I thought I was giving the exec at the network all the information he/she needed to make an informed decision about my show. What I was doing was giving them all the ammunition he or she needed to say, "No." It was a lesson hard learned. I slapped myself and changed my strategy in year two.

The idea of going hard in year two, facing my demons and doing what gave me nightmares was daunting. However, I did it with the help of some talented folks who also were squaring-up to pitch for the first time. I learned a few important lessons that year.

    1.   Know your logline so well you can repeat it in your sleep. To help you know it, keep it short and simple where possible.
    2.   Make sure your logline tells a story. It's the first impression the executive gets of your project. It's difficult to come back from a dismal start if your logline is weak.
    3.   Know your story, your character and their motivations so well that there's no question that can stump you because you KNOW exactly how the characters will act/react.
    4.   And most importantly, know what specific visual, element or set piece of your concept the network is excited about.

Item #4 became super important. If you have a very strong idea you must know what element of your concept the network is mostly responding to. You must bring that piece to the forefront of your pitch. It's smart to build or rebuild your story around that idea and hold fast to it in your pitch. If the logline says "A" and the network brings you in to pitch "A", but you pitch "B and C" instead, it feels like the old bait & switch routine and you lose credibility.

I've learned to spot that logline element in concepts brought to me. I've been fairly successful at getting in the door by retooling the logline pitch. Last year, out of 70+ pitches at the Great American Pitchfest I found two pitches that contained elements I thought were on-brand for two different networks. After some retooling, reimagining and a complete rewrite of the concept, we got two network TV meetings. All we needed to do was go to the meeting pitch the logline they were expecting and tell the story they were expecting.

We didn't do that because the writer I was working with went back to his old story right there in the meeting.

Dude, we talked about this...

After months of rehearsing and my weekly reiterations that we had to pitch the element that got us through the door, dude walked in there and pitched the same old show that I told him we **weren't** doing. The pitch was so full of details, minutiae, psychology and sociological elements it was boring. Even I was falling asleep, and I could see the two executives' eyes glaze over.

We'd talked about this several times. I told him exactly what I submitted in the pitch logline. I warned him that deviating from that idea -- particularly when it is the idea that got us the meeting -- was a bad idea. Time and time again, over Skype calls and phone calls he agreed to tone it back and focus on this particular element of the pitch. He said he understood, but in the end, another story was calling his name like a Siren song and he went crashing into the rocks.

But I get it. He was emotionally attached to his original idea and he'd built this entire world around the concept. It didn't matter that he was sitting in a network TV exec's office for the first time and they were desperate to hear something good. It didn't matter that we **had** something good to tell them. It didn't matter that he was at the forefront of a day that could have changed his life forever. What mattered to him was that he liked his original idea better. I tried to explain to him that the world he created was science-y by nature (Sci-Fi) and the very specific ideas and ideals would benefit the show -- once it's on the air! But those ideas would kill the pitch meeting. And they did.

The main purpose of any network TV meeting is not to sell the show. It seldom happens. The main purpose is to get to the next meeting. And on to the next. And the next... until it **does** sell, or you're told, "No thank you."

Unfortunately, my friend could not let go of his sociological science experiment long enough to avoid self-sabotage. I interrupted him after a while and tried to get us back on track in the meeting. I'd see a glimmer in the execs' eyes, but then my writer friend would drone on about sociological details. I watched the project crash and burn right in front of my eyes. It was a shame because it was a good project and lots of cool potential to dazzle and mystify, like LOST. The writer was a nice guy. But I cannot work with him.

IDEAS ARE STILL IDEAL

May 29, 2016

It's been far too long since my last post.

However, despite the absence of words here on my blog, there has been a lot of movement and action behind the scenes.

A week ago, Sunday, I attended, my 4th Pitchfest with the Great American Pitchfest -- now called the Scriptfest. One of my producing partners, Ramona, came down from Northern Cal to lend an ear to the pitches were ready to hear. This time the event was much slower than usual and I attribute that to an updated prod company bio I added to the GAPF directory. In it I stated that I was primarily interested in television concepts and pilots, particularly Sci-Fi dramas or a series with a new or fresh take on procedurals.

Aside from the endless stream of time travel and supernatural/alternate universe stories, there were some intriguing concepts that caught my attention. I've gone through the 50 or so projects and narrowed them down to 12 that I want to take a closer look at.

Besides that side of the business, lest I forget, I am a creative too. I've been reworking some under-developed projects and developing brand new ideas too. One project that I am particularly excited about is a an idea the network loved when I pitched it but passed because the it "stepped on the toes" of another project they were heavily invested in -- which has since been delayed and now canceled.

Some of you may know it, it was called "Heartbreak." I hope to get these proposals out and into the network's hands by the end of June.

I'm also waiting to hear from a potential agent who's reviewing an unscripted proposal developed by another producing partner, Dionna (from Atlanta) and I. I love this project and it's been pitched before, but we hope to get a more receptive audience next time :)

Lastly, this summer I expect to pick-up where I left-off and continue writing my epic sci-fi period fantasy novel.

WHERE WE ARE TODAY

May 2018

Today I am working more strategically, but still within the realm of TV land. Most of my contacts at the network have moved on to other networks or gotten out of the business. Many of the people I worked with and helped get their first pitch meeting with a network executive are no longer interested in writing for TV. Many of whom I haven't spoken to in years. Unfortunately, that is the way things are in this business.

I have worked with writers, directors, producers, composers, fellow filmmakers, and many actors. In some cases the projects I've done with these folks have helped launch their careers in the industry. Nevertheless, when the work ceases, often the collaboration ceases as well. Some relationships cannot withstand the lull. Sometimes it's weird to see an old friend chat it up on social media, talking about new friendships *ad nauseum*, when he hasn't responded to anything you've put out there.

Nevertheless, you have to keep moving. That said, I'm still writing and I always will. Writing is the core of who I am.

Recently I finished my second book, **The Gray Melia** after I completed **A Perfect Weapon** aka **Deterrence Theory**. I'm working on a third book, a sci-fi original called **Demigods**. Writing novels has been a liberating experience. I've chosen to adapt my previous screenplays and the ability to write without consequence or fear of confining literary real estate (room on the page) is the best feeling ever. Scenes, sequences and set pieces that I've surgically extracted from my screenplays because there wasn't enough space has magically been re-woven into the fabric of my stories. Every screenwriter who has ever had to cut pages of his or her work to conform to industry standard formats should try adaptation.

Currently I am knee-deep in an amazing collaboration with a friend on a script for a Christmas-themed TV movie. A producer is already interested in developing the project. The experience continues to be drama-free and ego-free, with mutual goal of using this project as a launching pad for other projects. We are already considering a second script collaboration.

I've limited my partnerships to a chosen few. Most happen to be in the unscripted and/or reality TV side of the business, which works well because the area is not one of my strengths. I am mostly flying solo on the TV series writing side. It has been difficult to find a long term partner who wants to write – and writing means sacrifice.

My friend in New York continues to inspire me to return to my indie filmmaking roots, so perhaps there is a low-budget film project for me on the horizon.

I hope to catch a tiger by the tail again sometime soon. I am sure I will. Persistence counts. Hopefully it will not take four years again as it took for me to secure my first TV deals.

But that's a story for another book (hint hint).